Also by Anne Gorrick

Kyotologic

ANNE GORRICK

I-Formation

Book 1

Shearsman Books
Exeter

Published in the United Kingdom in 2010 by
Shearsman Books Ltd
58 Velwell Road
Exeter EX4 4LD

ISBN 978-1-84861-118-4

Acknowledgments
Some of these poems have previously appeared in the following journals:

*Coconut, Copper Nickel, Hunger Magazine, Otoliths, Peaches and Bats, Shearsman,
Situation, Sugar Mule,* and *word for/word*

The May Garden was anthologized in
The Bedside Guide to No Tell Motel – Second Floor (No Tell Press, 2007).

This book would not exist were it not for the generous assistance of Robert Kelly
and Maryrose Larkin. 10,000 thanks to Peter Genovese for the shelter he creates to
write beneath—he is always next to me in the garden.

Thanks also to Geof Huth and Sam Lohmann for their astute
editorial and proofreading eyes.

Contents

Her Site of Reversible Destiny

The February Garden	13
The March Garden	18
The April Garden	22
The May Garden	24
The June Garden	26
The July Garden	30
The August Garden	36
The September Garden	38
The October Garden	43

The Michelangelo Variations

Pietà	53
Creation of Adam	60
Creation of Eve / The Crucifixion of Peter	68
Night	80

For Margaret Powell (Pavel) Murzenski
(1916–2004)

Something has wreckt the world I am in

I think I have wreckt
    the world I am in.
It is beautiful.

—Robert Duncan
from *A Song from the Structures of Rime Ringing as the Poet Paul Celan Sings*,
in **Ground Work**

HER SITE OF REVERSIBLE DESTINY

The February Garden

How much of her need per ton of work?
The attraction to first flowers constrained
Peter typed the maple trees out his fingers, pale as feet
These five large lilies will throw their
singular stink around one evening in August

Factory lists for Maria's gardens
its years counted out in azaleas and countries
an Indian pink year
A garden's borders are its thoughts
It should feel like a separating world
and we incompletely still inside that
The maple unexpectedly teaches the snow about spring
Lilies like handles receive our hands cordially
To be red in the corn, in the need to divide
Five regale lilies as pale as feet
August spiked in red surpluses
thus the retention and will be subtle it will be
Taxes like eggshells, his breath like Chinese rhubarb

A factory list for the Maria Garten
If thought edges the garden, then azaleas establish this year
The garden should believe in its own separateness
Not to spray However around, but
handhas unexpectedly the snow, the maple
Five slat-footed lilies in the Pink
throw their smell over August's spiky evenings, surpluses
In February, a holding back to receive
a piece of sea Kohl on the tongue

A factory list establishes the edge of a walled garden
When thought edges necessity in azaleas
As for the garden, it tries to force her to believe in other worldly beings

that are formed imperfectly
She occurs never in order
Consider that, but first the charm seems unlimited
an excess opposed to the expectation of his hands
which have been applied with snow

> Spring comes in a barking voice, in steering wheels and lilies
> Sincerity included excessively: the lily flower, red like corn
> Our certainties divided, a necessity received and had
> In dignity the lily with slatted feet
> growing largely pink because of red
> To throw around the smell of respect in spiked surpluses:
> sea coal, Chinese rhubarb
> the broken shells of eggs and taxes

This garden's factory tried to establish an edge
our necessity attain each ton
In order to envelop this year in India and azalea
form is not assuredly in angered flesh
Inside order assuredly, spare to that
Intelligence inside his hands opposes the eye's expectation
Weeks that bark beyond excess

> Flowers deep red, the color of corn: the winter sun setting
> Dignified she in evening-regard to her surpluses
> Order broken and thrown
> Aluminum and because
> deep red it grows five things pink colored
> Evening imagines regale lilies, a moon's grudge
> Reason returns underground to property
> A Chinese kind of rhubarb, and the cross it receives
> the graded entrances of infants and ocean coal
> Suction, projectile, taxed

In order to wrap need up in a year
In order to establish herself in azalea and India
without hanging from the tree of fleshed anger

Imperfect belief undoubtedly in spare parts
His intelligent hands barked in excess, in weeks
The lilies finished her in the same way
Method differs from hours
from ocean and aspiration

      In permanent attrition, at arm's length
      when the anger in flesh in not allowed the doubt in
           lacquered trees
      An excessive quantity to be colored in dark red
      This kind of China accepts
      categories of entered ambitions written in sea coal
      The tax on spherical objects

The garden's attrition along its walls
its uses beneath paper
The garden at work on the idea of itself
Each year, filled with a metric ton of necessity
the distances measured in arms' lengths
To establish a garden in the shape of Maria
whose doubts arrive in Indian azalea
the color of irritated meat vented from fact

      Flower of first limited enchantments
      Not that this starts in a pair of intelligent hands opposed
           to sound
      The look of hope roared in excess
      The maples examine spring
      In the fist of the iris, sincerity in an extreme amount
           of coloring
      The reds turn black in accepted necessities
      Reduction of smells and play, an aluminum request
      because the red blackness stops increasing
      the rose color of the place
      Plates of great iris quicken like hours or resentment

In the durable places of abrasion, walls read like paper
The garden of Maria manufactures another person
another country, like India in the form of azaleas
Doubts waived, provoked meat, marks in the garden form us
The personnel attached to form
The intelligence in his hands becomes the opposite of clay
roared abundance inside weeks, trees marked by examination
The reduction inside smell follows aluminum
a red density recedes to rose
Each hour changed into an automobile
ambition in the form of the sea or coal
These are unfounded categories in the garden

        A place of enterprise and endurance
        Maria's garden: that thing on paper drawn until the edge
        Abandon doubts of order, the year comes in packages
        The edge of Maria's garden becomes India arriving
        induced to separate into azaleas
        Signs attached to each person, spare us excess and bloom
        Time on the side of this condition called "clay" or "desire"
        abundant inside the unknown weeks that roar with
                intelligence
        Inside his hands: wood and the inspection for signs
        Imagine finishing in reddened editions
        An abundance shown in her which decreases the scent
                of the I
        Hours pass like automobiles
        we practice moderate amounts of reason
        Reason resets the surfaces of possibility
        The coal seas of ambition, taxes

We endure paper edges, intervaled burdens
Meat hangs from the trees, indications attached, a person forms
An excess of humanity, spared desire, weak and roaring
The extreme colors of lilies against the summer
Peeled to a standstill, petals like footprints
a questionable abundance imagines the finish

The aluminum demands of reason
The hours between you and an automobile
degrees in centigrade listed whole
Sea coal sheds its ambitious profile

        Petals transported in debatable manners
        risked necessity
        an imagined covering, a visible garden in aluminum
        The ocean spills like coal smoke over China
        or arguments over taxes

The frayed resistance in paper: afterwords
Eight intervals of difficulty
each like a metric ton of torn paper edges
A suspicious armature: this year packed up like meat
Approval the color of sheep
to presuppose a need for risk and small flags
When your cereal is dark red and divides
When place is reduced inside skin
Lily petals fall in February's imagined summer
Each hour between you and the car ticks off a risk
Coal from the ocean inverted into argument

        Paper soaked in alcohol along the edges
        Gardens marked in India
        Children and coal in the ocean of ambition
        transported throughout the world
        like a discussion of taxes

The March Garden

form   Who wouldn't say that factories keep an order
              against depression or gardening?
with   Going to bed with a book in the garden . . .
              The omnipresent hot grey mud called a "backyard"
              The last years have been weedy
              I will have to kill a book of work, cover it in newspaper
benign   Still. These kisses are me thinking
              He can choke her single form with benign negligence
              The morning is unsure that the hollyhocks will survive it
              Vague signs, her aconite nape, the downside of winter
negligence   Jonquils emergent, unpeel the garden from its winter

Blowout and success almost stops
the hydrangeas as if good, as if the year could be classified as "good"
Hollyhocks did not affirm the survival of her damaged sternum
Vague symbols attached to winter
Saffron crocus, jonquils urgent
The iris has not yet skinned the winter off the rock garden

in   Morning stuns the depressed garden
              The question always: bed or books?
              Indoor heat omnipresent, as pessimistic as a cement well
              The work spreads out to kill a year, like an affair
carelessness Any leaves behind her are unfortunate truth
              Canned good are never as good as an affair
              something blown like success or perhaps
              Every hydrangea is as good as a classified year
only   The heart is a vague symbol, as vague as these recent
                        winters

There is a range of morning that weakens the garden
Factories maintain the bed with thoughts of books in a garden
The beds in the front yard spread with murder

An excess occurs like news
The leaf cover in the period of a year
Still. You go away with unfortunate truth

then   As for her, she's a very large numeral that continues to
                  increase
              Anxious, the possible morning, kissed to consider
              Partial only has something against her
the   In success justly to be careless, indistinct symbols
              If monkshood, then the unbent winter
              Upside the saffron crocus is jonquil urgent
unbent   The first small sized iris, their frantic skin

The garden is somewhat weakened by arrangement
Cement and telephones are omnipresent
The end to threaten a central dissemination of the murderous bed
I must invest the work with any excess I have
The years measured in leaves and newspapers
Still, the you with me in consequence of unhappy truths

uncommonly   How much of her is simply the result of grand numerals?
              An increase kissed in possible mornings
              Partial cast into perhaps
              Form neglects to pierce her in tin
              Everything is uncommonly hydrangea good
hydrangea   The center of the wound is the will, indistinct symbols
              Winter unbent with aconite
              under a layer of winter monks. Still there are some flowers
              The underside of saffron: jonquil urgent
good   The first skins, frantic-sized, an iris unpeeled

The end of arrangement
released from families, beds, factories, from books
The cuts are pessimistic, built with cement
a telephone end threatened
A central diffusion over a fatal bed, periodical excess
To what number will she increase?

Impatient with kisses: the morning
Have you considered just how much having an I costs?

The   Partial is never only something to him
                neglected tournaments, the rare good in hydrangeas
Japan   This health which must classify this year
                The Japan of functions, the correct applications of wood
                      and when
                The winter slackened with aconite, layers of monks
of   The winter ceases to continue
                Saffron upstream, jonquils pressed
functions   The first skins in the rock garden

Morning: the end of arrangement
The pessimism in cement
noting that smallness is almost absence
The fatal bed invested with days
She or the excess
Funeral periodicals in the duration of a year
Grudge increased with morning, spared needs
The silence is graded
Intelligences peel from the hollyhocks
The extra prize of will
Loosened from sleep, aconite layered with winter monks
Indistinct symbols stand in for winter
"Always" flowers, jonquils pressed high
The iris in first skins, limitlessly small, unpeeled

The   A factory-intended end of arrangement
                Pessimism adheres to a small absence
end   The days collapse into a fatal bed, invests in time
                Magazines and funerals:
of   quite hydrangea!
                A bowl dried with danger
                She loosens her neck from winter's monks
arrangement A screen of jonquils in place of first skins, limitlessly

Beds are systemic arrangements of morning
The edges of day tacked with funerals, entirely a book
The public land that sits down with you attached
You are ardent with deformation
something adhered to pessimism that has an absent mouth
Days anteriorly with funerals and magazines
As if time could rescue her
from morning and its attendant emergencies
The dangers inherent in carrying around other people's sleep
The I thrown together excessively with jonquils at odd angles

ardently   Morning reorganizes weakly around a family or a factory
                  The books or public earth planned
                  ardently toward deformation
                  She feeds adhesions and pessimism into an absent mouth
                  Buckets filled with funerals, days, uniforms
toward   Height and the possibility of leaving
                  shoot the excess that divides us
                  The excessive price of sleep against her neck
                  Monks in winter begin to look to her like liberations
                  The sign that is the calm continuation of winter, indistinct
deformation   Hours, skins, stones form a screen, limitlessly

The April Garden

The sky's miracles gaze into her thinness
Weeping: what she does to give the days form
Because Shaolin gave me "Colette" in roses
The garden takes in her greening arms
willful, ancient wood narcissus
Spring's shadows fall into their fire

        Guinea hens: obstinate and strange
        The ancient yellow of narcissus in April woods

That which has extraordinarily expanded is recently thin
Crying is what makes the days occur now
The old yellow narcissus is intentionally strange in the wood
Photography lodges itself into one of her weekends
It's purpose? To stand still very quickly

        Star of many miracles A and as for me
        sometimes you'd think I'm composed
        entirely of my own screaming
        Grandmother: where we were large once

Cancer peels her into thinness
Each day now is a cinder
Darwin criticizes her lips
a pink impression, yellowed pages
Aluminum silk, cancer silver
She fasts and stands as though inside glass beads

        The cancer believes in itself
        Regard the many, many stars in her
        "Colette" knows the essential color of roses
        The writer believes firmly, yet it does not happen
        Quiet inside an aluminum book

Consider stars, their vapor whistles
how they spread out their thoughts across the night
in our shouts, our affliction
How do you know the true color of roses?

>Darwin's own blood spills
>Changed yellows
>I am installed inside a photograph
>for the duration of one weekend
>The rope colored crown
>Movement takes place in glass granules

The belief that time exists completely for cancer
The skin end of a dog
As for me, the stars are steam considered
The rose whose belief is secure

>When knowing does not happen
>Green: a fact which waits around for tulips
>When fairness first changes
>I fast from silver
>The aluminum silks of cancer
>their glass particulates
>engaged in movement, acquisition

The May Garden

A   That calcium moon
                 passes in and out of clouds
nightmare   bleached with impatience
                 If the rest of the sky
                 dark purple and caustically
                 then a leather garden
in   The green delivers chrome plate
                 a nightmare in enamel
                 I can sit inside it later and tremble
enamel   when August blows hotly across my skin

Kissed at the end of night, one side ached
A Stangl jug filled with lilacs
white with nuances
The azaleas are dark crimson and spiky
as if they carry in their casual hands
high boots in black patent leather
A garden to send nightmares that come in chromium and lacquer
The heliotrope is vanilla smeared, a consolation prize

floating   I have more installations
                 that must be carried out this weekend
                 The stone sink to the shade garden
                 must be planted with impatience
off   rose and blank under heavily nuanced shade
                 Must celebrate "Colette" around the azaleas
the   I want a black garden someday, a leaning garden
                 an S&M garden
                 A garden where I can send nightmares that come
river   floating off the river

This calcium month of cloud entrances and exits
Rather you should place this weekend within me
There are many plants
their irritation shiny in pink and white

As for me "of garden; Black"
The fact that a garden often desires plants
a garden that sends the unpleasant impression of command
Dignity passes from one sector of my skin into another
I am possible to tremble
As a reward of comfort, you move into shade

Digital   Where is that side of night that smells like Stangl filled
                    with lilacs, achingly?
in their   This is the calcium month (cloudcover)
               Digital in their magenta: "Pink Delight;" Hole
               It is a black starting with a shovel
magenta   That it establishes, the facts want me in leather

I consider the house an extremity
the focal point of a lateral night
Difference and puncture cross the skin
In ardors of azalea, wildness arisen
The night will often load blackness onto another color
Dignity passes for the hot suction of our skins

An   The fucking as a form of extremity
               across the lateral night
               Stangl lilac-white achingly
irritation   Then I went back into the house
               urged largely by a slow night of fucking
               A weekend went wrong inside me
that   Foxgloves seemed to be numbered individually
               another joy in pink, in buddleia, in self-deprecation
               An irritation that shines in pink and white under heavy
                    shade
shines   A consolation prize in this vanilla scented heaven

That time in me went toward the house
Cloud wild, ragged days into rags
The garden will be black someday
and I will send in the nightmare: chrome and lacquer

The June Garden

and   A one-note garden
                  with a stone sink filled with eyelets flowering
                  The pinks that come before illness
                  Insouciant beauties increase my idea of pink every day
false   and false pink oranges, savage as a sugar refinery
                  Their canes bend completely
                  covered in scented luminous pink lemons pink
pink   It is almost too, and also never
                  Chocolate sheets in deep blue flowers
oranges   So much about the garden takes always

Rockets shaped like women
bright in shade
The sink garden bitten off in coral fragments
False orange and wildness make the world smell like candy
their sticks become arch-shaped, completely lemon bright pink
At present no place
almost to be remaindered sufficiently

is   It is never that
                  The increase of small things, irregularly large
never   The root cover was done in re-pink
                  The flowers of your deep blue ends in ajuga
that   You permanently exclude concern

Dame's rocket at that cat clamping place
and roses spiced with tented spiders
Let us extend the mean term of Pink each day
It is nearly too much, and nevertheless it is not enough
Lazy around the yard on and on and away
Productive nothing amounts to too
but the increase of small things finally in large things
The morning in love with the spread of ajuga
Chocolate skipped over the deep blue flowers
As much as over in garden work takes always

in   The back court looks lovably in rocketry luminous
                   Coral bells, catnip, and spidery malt liquor bottles
rocketry   The roses change crazily in front of us
                   expand my concept of pink daily
                   Disguised in orange: a likely candy
luminous   The canes arched in lemon quilted stems

The multiplication of minor matters
in final total importance
covered the tree roots in peony pink
Morning in love with dissemination
Dark blue conclusions, chocolate leaves
engaged to forever extremely in need

in   The garden writes its own notes
                   in dame's rocket luminous
                   in masked trees, water gutters, choral bells
masked   The changes in pink you find in an ill person's front parts
                   It expands my rose one, the idea to be daily
trees   All the world a probable candy risen in her
                   The canes in arc and quilt
water   Age is almost too much, sufficiently never
                   Puttered in the yard and all weekends
                   the lesser total of substance and multiplication finally
gutters   The garden forever chained to need

Rockets in luminous injury
Water guttered in chinensis
Changes in the pinks of a person, beauty insouciant
It increases my rosy idea of being daily
Orange pink and savage makes him feel that
the world is a probable sugar refinery

Sheets   Eiderdown in lemon arcs, in brilliant pink if increased
                   Age is almost too much, sufficiently never
if   The multiplication of finally
                   A full fifth and charette

```
                    Morning in love with ajuga and diffusion
blue-dark           Sheets if blue-dark chocolate in conclusion
```

Our cuts look at us loveably
Bright injuries in gardened template
Wild marks on the world refined
I have necessity approximately
Lemon this bright pink
Surfaces atomize covered in blue-dark
chocolate in summary of the flowers
Exclusion attaches

```
bright              Ardent notes at the back of the mouth
                    come out as a garden
                    The yard is bright with injury
with                Signs found in wildness and orange roses
                    belief in the sugar spirit place increases
injury              conceptual as a daily newspaper
                    There may there be a world. It rose
                    As for me, a 4 o'clock necessity
                    A lemon around this scent of bright pink
                    Tired very for the sake of, that becomes, you ask, is
Signs               The tomorrow part spread in front of the ajuga
                    atomization as a form of love, used
                    In summary, a flowered dark cover
found               on the upper surfaces of the garden
```

Ardent with fame lodged in your mouth: the garden
Hours wound like rockets in luminous template
Signs are increased in wildness
a sugared spirit, a newspapered world
In order possessing this color in luminous rose
my hatred is sufficient in these
only the front parts of tomorrow
When love is atomized in chocolate blue summary
The fact that is worked over the advanced surfaces of the garden
A lot and necessary, this exclusion

Until   The garden is ardent as fame in her mouth
             hours shapes like beautiful A's
reason   Wounds rocket over her luminous wooded groups
             Orange sampled wildly in place of sugar
is   Until reason is mine
             One of lemon around
mine   rose in eider totally in order

Age is almost never sufficient until there is more age
The weeks end in her extremities
The first parts of morning atomized
with love used for That
Chocolate in summary of that blue-dark covering
fixed with ajuga, necessity excluded and always
Facts at work on the garden's surfaces

The July Garden

Fireworks	The white screen of another month resembles
	the white out of her fingers
are	while her temperature falls. Still
	Made madnesses on delicacy
a	The peonies bankrupting, silver plated
	A quarter of July cut into holidays
	The beach inside an old house, and the fireworks' brief
	garden
brief	Out of the ocean: miles
	or a garden almost completely played out
	except for the curiosities of goosenecks
garden	The oak still splendid: red with bees

The screen is another month in front of her
because it resembles taste
Her fingers move out of this computed white
The silver belly of mental disorders in elegance:
the bankrupted farm
The jet fire in airplanes, a traveled king of allotters
The beach, like many old houses, has people and fireworks
pulled out of it like miles
overwhelming in its excess
In moth curiosity
daylilies and the jackmanii empty out July
In balsamed bee calms, forced weathers in red and magenta

Time	Temperature a pregnant falling, meant slowly. Still
	Many beds of iris rhyme with the elegance of a farm
	where flowers yesterday were white
resembles	or silver gone bankrupt
	The fire in the jetcraft of minor kings
	holidays plated with fireworks
first	The ocean pulls miles out of the old beach house
	In order to generate a larger spectacle

```
                    the garden sinks under loosestrife
glances             Curiosity remains in daylilies, empty if done


Another month fronted her
when time is similar to looking
She: temperature too inadequate to locate the I's whereabouts, slowly
The farm loftily spent silver: the peony bankrupted
Old houses and fireworks, the sea unraveling for miles
Carmine moths, in complete curiosity


or                  The months laid against one another
                    while time stops in her fingers
                    in white consequence
                    Still, if you become iridescent
silver              if the peonies in yesterday, then the silver dawn insolvent
                    Competition plates the king
                    Holiday's substantial beach
bankrupts           The sea pulled from its own miles
                    We trace words on the upturned throats of geese
                    Water gutters in paper majority
daybreak            Bees forced clearly for properties in red


A fat month in front of the I
Time because it is similar to whites and blacks
The ore in her finger movements
in white consequence
She is not full of her temperatures
whereabouts I, meaning slowly
assumed excavations
Expenditures understood yesterday possibly
The cause of silver for an agricultural factory


of                  Peonies declare daybreak bankrupt
                    A wild spray of airplane fire
                    Competition chooses which king to silverplate
a                   Suitable fireworks pull a mile out of the sea
                    The garden's waterdrain gutter in goose throat trace
```

First papers incomplete, the Jackmanii threaded through
daylilies
sea   The bees in forced product

One month of white screens inside
The hours a similar search for hazard
Wild in airplane gushing, excavated
The plating in competition peeled
Dawn in urgent inability which becomes declaration
to a white farm
Tablelands in gain and loss, it writes
The holidays peel from the hazards carried by July
The seashore longs for fireworks, suitable to stand in for miles
Trace knowledge at the throat, geese gutter in adjacent waters
First papers and rum
The jackmanni snaps off inside the daylilies
There the butterfly ends
In the beds, property is a clear ingredient
Red, and the car it pushed off

Small   The hours in risk initially
           The movement of her fingers stops
           at endangered interiors, unsatisfactory temperatures
still   Small, still: You
           become excavation, inert
           Plated in pressing incapacity
           which becomes the declaration in color
You   peeled off yesterday

Explosives, ground tables, risk
Profit and loss revise him
The holidays peeled and quartered
July carries interiors similar to seashores
An ocean in wish for a detonator ardently
The house sways in agreements
In order to be happy, compare risk
trace knowledge against the throats of Canadian geese

adjacent water gutters
First paper excludes him, remaindered in rum
Multiple Jackmanii broken far inside the daylilies
Property and risk are obligatory in red cars pushed off cliffs
certain ingredients released

In   Months compose her asymmetrically
       The shape of hours that taste like risk
       Her temperature is inadequate, meant slowly
the   Still, if we become iridescent in spent understanding
       How white was yesterday
       your perhaps formed in silver dawn avowed insolvent
         wildly
course of   Decided in fire: July
       a quarter in resemblance to a holiday
       The beach, many old houses corrected by fireworks
       The sea, pulled out of miles
competition: A cause for a larger illustration, exceeds in luck
       in sunken competition
       Substance traced at the throat of a goose
       a water garden incompletely made of paper
Her   The forced manner of characteristics

A white screen covers her
like hours that fall, like risk at the beginning
The movement of her fingers at his interiors
The I endangered by temperature, means the I insufficient
Always, the You becoming more nuanced
excavated, inserted
Wild and a plan of gushing
the incapacity, the pressure
Declaration in white to be peeled possibly
Groundtables of risk

Paper   At the night's seaside, there is so much ocean in July
       that burns like wishes detonating
       Happy in completed risk, traces of knowledge

	like the upturned throats of geese
	Gutter in adjacent water
excludes	Paper excludes us
	remaindered in rum, in multiple jackmanii
	The flower will break the distance between daylilies
	A butterfly inserted with property
	Obligatory released
us	Red and the car they pushed

There will be white screens and moths to cover her
in dresses that look like hours
The You delivered from nuance, excavation, introduction
It was wild to plan, and gush
in the process of competition, in selected orders
Descend as far as possible into pressure
The incapacity to descend into loss: she writes to it
Holidays made up of one quarter risk
The ocean desire burning and persona
Competition immersed in water, happy in its own completion
Locate traces of knowledge in the fluttering throat of adjacent waters
The distances conclude in compulsory reds

Small	The months in front of her like a screen
	Time tastes like danger, threatens the I
the	which was always intended to be small
	The nuances of excavation
wildness	The wildness in plans
	Him: the explosive that writes the farm
	A pure white declaration, the disabled power in pressure
in	There is an ocean which desires this house
	the thousands of external personalities of the seashore
plans	Commerce surpasses reason

Facts dampening in water, the search in it for the physical
The You excluded from first papers
The broken eye of the will in intervals, daylilies
the remaining ram liquor in plural jackmanii

Completed knowledge at your throat
We bring the quality of danger to the raw materials
mandatory in bees
Color the automobile red in order to harvest

when   Time tastes like beginning
                    She threatens insufficient temperature
                    The I, which is intended, is small
                    The farm writes in her a moment of pure declaration
                    Need and him: explosive
the   The farm where you write marks of pure declaration
                    In addition to holidays: forms, behaviors, the material July
                    One quarter of interior dangers are always similar
                    The ocean wishes for this very house
I   and a thousand external possibilities installed
                    on the edge of the sea, detonated
                    Danger competes when the I is happy
                    when the I surpasses reason
surpasses   Fact dead in the water
                    Here eyes are broken by his will
                    Daylilies carry luck at their throats
reason   Bees made compulsory against a red harvest

The August Garden

Even   A Japanese maple assembled from pennies
                   Three summers of hydrangeatotal: tit-high brown
                   heart splittingly
my   In wind, hot light and gold
                   sunk into the green of August
                   Even my conscience gardens
conscience   The back deck is a ship filled with pink germaniums
                   the pink of a sugar refinery
                   White alyssum rubs against an intelligent blue
gardens   A germination factory!

The small garden has shifted from the I
to that of the entire world
Hydrangeas tit-high: pink brown and blue
When color is a verb
Not much the flowers
in addition the heart is wonderful splittingly

Azaleas are small in accumulation
The azalea spring is a type of factory
The center splendid splittingly

Fact: Hours are amended and clear
                   August's gold sunk inside green
it will   Fact: it will come out and snap off by winter
                   The garden dozes beside its reputation
come   Shepherd's Purse floats over deep-red, top dark
                   Colors freeze to death in the christophii allium
out   Gorgeous with hazard

We open up the hours
Cyan, the salvia, ascension
Deep red and high dark
A confidential room open for suggestions

The end of apprehend
Gorgeous with intelligence and danger

Check against the authoritative text
and you will find the hour has opened
the gold sunk into an internal green
Facts are exterior, gasps

are   Controls put in place against
                the found text, the open hour
descended   In August, the wind and the gold
                are descended from all forms of green
from all   Blue-dark, fresh white
                Green noises rearrange into dark red by night
forms   The Japanese maple: an attempt at possibility
                and its factory of subordinate components
of   Compare the tree to the idea that germinates it
green   Its green intelligence is splittingly dangerous

The September Garden

She has an appointment with geologic time
Only when time is disentangled from will
will we know for sure
a principal word, newly learned: anaclitic
Try to sew a name into the linen sky
Indigo. Can I sew this autumn into her greasy feathers?
I am covered in red inkdarks
The maple fishes for cream
something drawn from digital images:
a bouquet in late pink

The twilight of common stags and deerlings
browsing on bad grasses
She continues to try to keep her heart
from falling out
Catch it and reinstall it, duct tape to hold it

Anaclitic: "on the magnitude which tilts"
Unless there are jonquils that tilt on geology
we possess the joke
Time disentangled from indigo
The sky broken from its facts
Named easily: "blue sewn cloth"
I am covered in ink red darknesses
The cracks in her bed arrive like days
To be pulled out from something like shock
The weekend's bouquet of slow pinks
Grasses seen from the Observatory:
the common male deer browsing, a deerling

She is anointed with geologic time
Words evenly learned
"Anaclitic"—a word that tilts
Time is a straight line untangled

which concerns us, really
The sky is a poor attempt at fact
Names sewn easily into this blue cloth
Her feathers are covered in red ink

        A barrier to fishings and cream
        Distances jump on her bed, mosquito warnings
        The grass is dried digitally
        The weekend is a bouquet of slow pink
        The common male, his rot wild, grazing
        and the deerling narrowly
        Facts cover her central trunk
        Prevented, she gets caught at high volume

In equal personage: the dog
Anaclitic: the size of the slant
The life in question: a matter of the surplus in jokes
The hour resolves itself exactly
How easily his name falls out of her clothing
read like a piece of green onion sewn
The imperfect facts in an indigo sky
She is me deep in red ink
She sleeps against a wall
Fishings and cream are a matter of concern
Their relationship is warned by mosquitos and tincans
She spits a digital silence into bad grasses
Characters graze on paper, adjacent waters

        The promised jokes in geologic characteristics
        We are accurately solved only by hours
        Easily in onion sutures, her studying is not perfect
        Names fall from her clothes
        hereupon fact in indigo
        Her spatial canisters, mosquito-warned, in digital silence
        The slow pink color in a bouquet of dogflowers
        Characters narrowly rot, eat paper carelessly
        Her skeleton makes an attempt at fact

The dog is educated in onion joinings
knows her name in his fur
On top of facts, an indigo I
tinplated boxes full of mosquitos in numerical quiet
informed by duplicate vibrations, negligences consumed
Characters laid on bleached grasses, the tentative skeletal line
She seizes and obtains facts attached to adjacent waters

        The baby's suspicion of new life
        She has an excess of that I substance
        The jokes in her promises
        The hours constantly revise themselves in her
        Study is not a perfect nomination of her clothes
        an indigo superior to fact

Jump on the bed, ours, an interest in fish
Creams stop asking at all
Mosquitos in a tinplated box
an informed metal is dangerous to external intelligence
The numerical will of quiet
duplicated in bad grams
The negligent wild of the common male deer
Mine this, mine central mine
closes a tentative skeletal line, apprehended

        Who is equal to the dog's test in educating
        her as an important person
        "Anaclitic:" a downhill-sized word
        We have in us a surplus of age
        geologic characteristics promised in jokes
        That I kind of matter
        Upper and lower garments nominate autumn
        easily as the winner
        The indigo I in leaf flag
        The ore is red, inked with density
        jumps the wall around her bed

Barrier fish and cream requesting, all extremely
The box-shaped space, mosquito box, tinplating this news
Wishes duplicated as quiet digital vibrations
Bouquets of slow flowers like weekends, like dogs
The I continues blanching its character
in narrow bad comments
Mother-discovered negligence
mines an ore close to the skeleton
Pipe delivery, magnetic tape

       The dog tests the sloping size of words like "anaclitic"
       We are a form of surplus
       Affairs fucked to dresses and autumn appointed
       an indigo sky
       A red ore jumps on the bed
       interested in barrier fish
       interested in cream, fast metals
       the copied vibration of the calm digital will
       Stations bleached, commented away
       The wild generals and discovered carelessness
       The ore closes in on the skeleton, fact actually
       bolting devices seized by magnetic tape

She has the joke of occurrence in her
Empty physical interest unique to our surplus
Our clothes are investigated, a season of hair
Fish jump in her bed
a bed that interests the wall
where cream and all materials are bitter
Intelligence becomes external to craving
She has a dangerous relationship to the crying metals
Digital calm, slow weekends that look like dogs
Mountains bleached badly with generals
Wildness and carelessness search her character
for deer, ore, device and range, lock and bolt

The test of the dog to the very important
an inclination to correspondence
He supports the doubt of this place
The decisive time, the physical interest he takes in joinings
An indigo falls out of the sky
She takes a mineral jump

Fish, and the barrier, and the bed which interests the wall
A bouquet he chooses made of weekends and dogs
Generals whiten the mountains
Graspings united with mineral contiguous
for your tape recorded delivery

Shadows are the mother of all dice
an anaclitic case for depth
We only have jokes and emptiness
physical interest and lightbulbs
dresses: sized, indigo
Until that jump, take control of the flesh: mineral red
many bitters in cream
The vibration of the digital and then calm
The generals seriously whiten those mountains with letters
The wildness in dice
in commitments and negligence
Lines on our chassis sluice mineral earned characters
Graspings, devices, that the contiguous is tape recorded
A photocopy of water and a deer taped to it

The October Garden

Our first true freezing
by the time the sheets hang in addition to the leaves
I supervise the landscape
There have been very few distinguishable reds this year
Facts linger in the Japanese maples
"Slap me red"
The hydrangeas turn to paper
pale and luminous
The birds devour the crimson seed heads
The sky divided multiply by a tree

The year is few and red under enormous rain
as soon divides itself
If I indicate a view, this year taken in small amounts
very mine amongst the You seen in red
A factual Japan applied with influences
in paper revolutions bright in an arc of salt
The birds below "Jeanne d'Arc"
the white of 300 Thalia swallows the wood immediately around him
That decreases were decreased

When autumn originates in rain and indicates
a view: German silver, deep red
Method dawns in a plate of hydrangeas
new jonquils the color of white cars

A medical exam in October, normality under an enormous rain
The enemy sees you completely in a German silver-plated place
which is red-dark
The facts outside of Japan: dishes of hydrangea
jonquils carved into the red-dark
The He is tall, next to a white car underneath a red pine
swallowing 300 Thalias
When he is divided from form

importance immediately ardently
This reduction of environments

        The interior of this year is enormous
        When German silver indicates sight in place
        of a dark red ore
        Papery, pale and luminous
        The Japanese fact applied to a tree
        "He will be red-dark, reliably believed"

Method shovels hydrangea, plates of jonquils
Belief in the firmly red-dark bulbs in electric lamps
The high crow and the white automobile
You under a red pine tree
300 established swallow's white
Thalia in components
Respect divided by form in love immediately, importantly
Environment in this reduction

        The You I write has changed
        Still inside the fall, an enormous rain
        Looking at this thing, this ore
        when the German enemy should cover the place
        with a silver that is also dark red
        A thin bright paper
        Japanese fact applied to function in wood, which is
                substance
        Securities stacked with red darknesses

Meaning in order to believe in electricity
The world prints an annual edition of 300 hydrangeas
The white automobile You
and being wooden the pine to be red
swallowed in white hostas where the jonquils are
When we are divided by form in certain decreases
immediately, seriously, decreased in love

October is the prosecuting attorney of these materials
In order to establish fact, we exchange seats
The I spreads out and it writes
Belief in enormous fires
in identical times, in Grace's Water Museum
An ore in place of obligation
The enemy of time and red
The paper, as dawn, thins
The Japanese fact as function applied to these trees
By him, an immediacy, the targets piled up
To believe in a lightbulb when it's dark
The jonquils point inside in inferior
white shedding of the blood curve
In love with reduction, the mother-body, in decrease

The I propagated outside and written
under enormous fires
Autumn rains mineral and obligation
Documentation is thin
The trees are applied to the sky above us
a considered directness, objects accumulate
jonquils swallowed in buttery light
The white autokinetic You
The pine tree and a spade divided
decreases in places of love
This mother-body, this reduction

The jurist in October
The I external, and he writes her
There will be enormous fires in this rain
Our interior autumns in regard to water
Expenditures, mineral final, obligation
When Germany is applied to the red of the thing
Documented together, we appear thin
Tasks accumulate alongside darkness

In concrete: she eats attainalities
A bright tuber of electrical light = sufficiency
Problems swallowed in walnut oil
The jonquils inside Jeanne d'Arc when she burned
an interior whiteness, blood oppression
Crow writing high crow
The white automatic kinetic You
swindled hydrangeas from a red pine

        Jurist, natural elements, examinations
        Minerals established instead of place
        The electric light is tubercular with obligation
        Tasks accumulate in responsibility
        The whiteness of jonquils, a blood oppression
        Crow high, a kinetic automatic target
        along the axis of a hydrangea
        The atmosphere diminishes leaving him on an axis divided

October is a material jurist
a place for ending mineral things
The obligation in him
German characters in red time
The crow has written in order to write
You swallow jonquils, pure white
He shines electric against concrete
The methods of resembling when she is systematically new
The atmosphere divides, decreases
On the axis of automatic motion: some hydrangeas

THE MICHELANGELO VARIATIONS

For PRG, my guide through the mechanical gardens . . .

If prayer means communication with the divinity, running at high speed is a prayer . . . One must snatch from the stars the secret of their stupefying, incomprehensible speed . . . Our female saints are the light and electromagnetic waves at 3x10 meters a second. The intoxication of great speeds in cars is nothing but the joy of feeling oneself fused with the only divinity.

—Filippo Marinetti,
"The New Religion—Morality of Speed," 1916

The nearer the automobile approaches its utilitarian ends, the more beautiful it becomes. That is, the vertical lines (which contrary to its purpose) dominated at its debut, it was ugly, and people kept buying horses . . . The necessity of speed lowered and elongated the car so that the horizontal lines, balanced by the curves, dominated: it became a perfect whole, logically organized for its purpose, and it was beautiful.

—Fernand Léger, "Aesthetics of the Machine:
The Manufactured Object, the Artisan, and the Artist," 1924

I think that cars today are almost the exact equivalent of the great Gothic cathedrals: I mean the supreme creation of an era, conceived with passion by unknown artists, and consumed in image if not in usage by a whole population which appropriates them as a purely magical object.

—Roland Barthes, "The New Citroën," 1957

Michelangelo's art is more abstract than 90 percent of the so-called "abstract" art ever produced in this country.

—Robert Smithson,
"What Really Spoils Michelangelo's Sculpture," 1966

Pietà

Mother wrap us in your thorns
sentence is open ground

It doesn't have to do with
the temperature of objects
but with propagation through the material

A dialect of flesh
A flat water
A mineral coil down the spine

All open ground is drawn across the back

* * *

A boy becoming a hill

and paid grid against the body

and you held in your arms

"Trim thy vine"

When Orpheus was a girl

Fetus lost its feathers to water

Its thin arms fold and mute

Dust devils siphon off what's left

* * *

The water in the river
is blue today:
an estuarine memory of the sea

A bucket in the smoke
a cup of coffee:
after visitation
all Mary needs
"Beyond the arm
daughter, you are born of apple
an experiment in autobiography"
Grief is time
How she got the girl back?
In the falcon's claw

* * *

Mary sits in her dull world

(the beginning of turn one)

Dress pulled up

The digestion of driver

God's whore

Knuckle-rage at humanity's insectal drive

Blood lifts to the ears first

Cars the sound of torn aluminum and sleep

disappear into dust

* * *

A string
across the chest
and you fell through the weather
before me
behind the waist
constructed from the house of stone
Here is a piece of leather
I am the music
I'd not considered
Wrap the broken vein around
like this
over the right shoulder
perfect for the sound of empty wood
Root to the chair
I am cut 13th century from cathedral stones

* * *

White drones smother the broken hive

The smell is 117 octane, perfectly burned

"Ah, the smell of money burning, the smell of it turning
into hot air"

Left alone with the radio on

Mary is in the grass now and

things are hurling through her

Fracture the asphalt with fast colors

Everything is coated in iodine and silver nitrate:

ambulance and snow

* * *

Am I simply machine and saying?
A "membrane to keep the death out?"
Before spoken
body is a rabbit's fission

Teeth turn word and blue on the ink pap

Copper's cataract and stagnant
curl and grown into soft azure ferns
down to the bone shaped as a triangle

I have so many questions my limbs curl naturally

Endmark is the tropical wing
drawn tightly to the body

Regrade the slope of ocean and memory
There is safety to existence
Waves curl in the head

* * *

"Root it not up yet"

Sky as the color of ice

sat in its water for a second and burned

Sort feathers from stalks in the Catholic night

whose sky was a plain of ice

"Cut it to the quick"

And you held a triangle to the grief-mouth

When he entered the hill

you blew geometries of faith

You took to the mouth and spoke it

* * *

The blood of the world
the wood of your neck
To consider floors to be
touch the vein on my ankle
Your lap is tattered
a velvet invitation

I prefer him as story:
glazed in ice that
fell off the mountain
cracked off like a shell

When the sun bled in the squall

"Watch that red car
The first curve of a woman
and then the kick of her hip"
A woman on her side

Wind in and around the body
You come from the place where sun equals snow
Surprise, indigenous

* * *

Fracture its black sticky night stretched out

The track's dark vein collapsed into

the accident night in the car

where vinyl seats made a thin church against winter's

scissoring metals

Flatness at the broken passions that travel

Someone walked up to me and told me the driver and I

were of the same face

the expression of "velocity as art"

* * *

In the state of Florida
Mary
god is catastrophe
something in the sky that burns

He swings her in a copper basket
She is the small field full of wild apples

The years are now more than mine
To touch those you call yours
We are all covered in ice
We search for evening in the colored atlas
You have one half hour

* * *

Choice becomes a contusion in time

a snow-song, a needle put to the sky

"Are you hunger itself?"

I sang and sing into Mary's cement robes

into the tattered aluminum belly

Are you hunger itself?

Ritual grass, ritual dirt

Creation of Adam

It might swim off

mouth and scattered

off the telephone poles

Osiris was sprayed on

the side of railroad cars

Text is the body torn from

The air is pieced from language found and made

that piece missing and bitten

* * *

As if a stone in a wall
has been broken into two, once luminous
Bulbs root in the spine
crowd out matter as thought

Dressed in lichen
(I'm even dressed)
Half a centimeter in a year
If you could call that flow
Sing to the children
who lie almost beyond name

Rotten feral Novembers
My shoes sing on the capstones

The bone plot on Maple Avenue
Bruise and escape

* * *

A cicada, a wasp's nest

a garden of aluminum, brass

All metals grow under the film

Apple-water pools in cement bowls

Carapace of the Lotus

hung from the ceiling, pack of

cigarettes opened with a screwdriver

Cut through with holes

each worn surface breaks into oil

* * *

There are no clues underwater:

The long dark hairs I curl in the palm
I find on the back of the chair:
thin roads that snap when traveled

The bloodcolored car
all bandaged with leaves

Each object is a star in an abstract constellation

There is a strange democracy of light here

I fuck to prevent your life's hinge
from splitting off the door

* * *

The ravenous sinews swallow up the joint

The terrible gristle of your confidences

They shot off the glass insulators

turning in the scaled waters

We are all pieces of aqua glass scattered

at the river's lips

* * *

Arm across the chest, palmed opposite hip
Bath. Sat closer to the fire

Carnivorous run
covered in nine years worth of lacquer
Drag carcass rags

Dry attic: the view is dogs
every belly split open, overripe
gilded in their luck-crop
Fold her into the earth's dark gape

He tells me, "twenty this morning"
I am numb and phantom in a…
I have braided this husk called hair
if you could call them wounds

In the woods, the hole was small
It were good grass
Leaves form a brittle hive over casual wounds

* * *

Eden is made of metal

Everything is a miracle of repair

Let's drink the sweet greens off your floors

Muscles in the cheek

a form of communion

My hands covered in chemical intimacies

When may I travel your reticent veins?

* * *

Braid this and this
Set in heavy atoms
(which fuse the air when we sleep)
I dreamed I ran through your evergreen house
collected cloth, and you let me

The tanks are almost empty
and the two of you float just beyond
the foot in front of me
That amazes
Cake and eat it too

If the odometer turns eleven eleven seven
it's a fine thing to sip off the night

* * *

An eroding memory of the geometric sea

cheek full of hope and falling teeth

Concoidal

Define a strand of hair as distance and forgiveness

Each muscle's rope is on the map

* * *

"Seven years" broke into two once luminous pieces
"Five months" lies on his back
waiting to be sung to
I read their ages to them with a finger

Root in my spine

They grow up through the skin shrunk off
eyes would be ragged
leaves bruised in their escape
Falling leaves hum their familiar
soon-to-be-gones. The red choke takes hold

Hollow out all sound

Waiting to be sung to

You will see mouth and stem grown one

* * *

Sapsmell of alcohol

Shot with holes, we become lighter

The crucial ounce shaved off

Twice you don't let me leave

Opacity and night

What has broken is sutured

What is original breathes additional limbs

but your body greys in the crucible jungle

* * *

Atlas without the effort
Atlas with lacquer in her eyes
Atlas whose civilization is sutured in muck
I'd place you in the sky so I could watch you:
a diamond on the scaffold
Turn from father into daughter

This blue sunless wraps me
in its thick cotton
its oxygen response

I have gone lacquer red into what I mistook for sky

Oxygen rapidly becomes though

* * *

Legs form a triple cross
lingered over asphalt as if

Look for a beam to cure on
On herself, the ghost of a fern
(renew the oils of protection)
Scared off the hill

Some sort of meager harvest curling
Stars burn into the soil

"Than anyone I ever knew"
The dogs bronze in their
The dogs return: cracking and bronze
The half-wolf comes home
snow-wild fur thickened by kill

* * *

Each muscle's rope spells

I set a dangerous foot in your

unnavigable seas

Form for a word

Gone next door

I am ragged and aqua

Touch the semi-circular side

I cradle these worn aqua thoughts

It might swim off

mouth and scattered

* * *

There are no genetic separations here
This is the season of iron

To try to remain in good shape:
Wash her of her sticky life
Waiting for a meal

Where a leg has separated from the body

Wring fur of its contents

Creation of Eve /
The Crucifixion of Peter

Bark-songs, rope-burn
arc of the light shorn
Admire the windsubtle movements of him
Interiors of a bowl
high-sided
A rim's line as seen

Swing in the recent and overnight

Hieroglyphics and sadness
Both a tree and a horse
high in a crop tree
until drunk ground shattered the legs
The hemp knot between
the thighs ripped clean

Climb a tree
Define a cessation of
woods by a piece of rope
Define ground by moving across it

He was indifferent from the cross

* * *

Eve traveled a biblical terrain
        Kiss around the numb to discover
        where feeling begins
        Sliver of a man as an arc of soap
        escapes the hands

Two people raked the hillside for old bottles
        countried dump needled with partials

He found a cocaine heart medicine
in the stone wall
What we all want:
reward for laying 10 yards of fitted slate

Eve in the body of Dorcas:

      bottle sown beneath leaves in spring
      Stand roadside in coltsfoot and salt
      "Now no one can make you afraid
      to be a sword on the bottom of the ocean
      left for 300 years"
      Orion and Simon, hunting, fishing
      in the stream of rust

Eve has Orion by the belt buckle
      and pulls him close
      The track rejects imperfection
      To become discreet at 200 miles an hour
      What is complete can vanish or be remade
      Zero chassis and strafe the cash crop

* * *

"Sky turns into a
glass of milk over St. Petersburg"
Absence of stars is a valentine
a massacre. Mongrol. Maker

Shoot snow from under the fingers
Unground the lingering world
The sky over Highland is a
glass of tea a man's been steeped in
Light orange, apricots
coffee and milk, thigh the color
inside the car you pulled him from

"The inside of the car turned red
and I one-handed him out"
Men pulling men from fire
Accident smiles in your bark face
and I chased you from the laurel

* * *

She is a stagnant shape of wind. She is ancient movement trapped.
Stand where the limb meets the trunk, back against the trunk as if
looking out a window. There are monkeys everywhere, grey and familiar
childhoods swinging around fat limbs, until one becomes trapped
upside down and the others rescue it. A man says, "why don't you try
it?" She can't. They must get down he says. They can't. So they jump.
She feels her pelvis disintegrate. She is in the grass now, smiling because
she can't believe she's alive and recently fucked.

* * *

Woken up from each rectangle

Crops seen from the air: parrotgreen

Unrib the self and rise off it

"Though her mouth has his speech"

Thought of birth by throat

Thought of corn in a field

There wasn't any blood, and then blood

The burn since has been

Game of pool played

with the table pushed against a wall

"A man, a god rather, inside a woman"

Ice chipped from the river in the form of Eve

* * *

Oil tanks collapse in Baltimore
      sun rusting the junk sky
      He hangs by his feet from a nail
      twirls as an artificial crow from a string
      a bare lightbulb off its cord
      Imperfection as a bald invitation
      Gather the ancient unusable wheat
      in the form of glass
      Seamless and aqua vessels for medicines

Eve crossed a starless sky
      to pencil him in at the belt
      Assemble the vast abstractions above
      A live bird hung at her throat
      Once grammar existed only in his face
      and then it went numb

Where are you when the oil tanks
      collapse and inflate?
      You are the boat that sails the waters above me
      Two people died on the asphalt circle
      of a minor world
      Leave blood on the hands
      it's beautiful there

* * *

The fragments of angels
enclosed nearly all

Hairy when young
but soon become hairless

With often leathery leaves
so as to resemble a cross
Sometimes have cork wings
Laced northern variety borealis
resembling turkey tracks in outline
Shaped as a shallow goblet

He appears loosely attached
A small tree, white, woolly
A bottomland tree

Some consider this to be only a variant

* * *

Naming the car:

"Angel-through-the-eye-of-the-needle, angel-eye, angle-iron." Cross
sections reveal angels to be flesh inside, blood outside. This is why
angels have red eyes.

* * *

Reduction of angles

Inappropriate forms of agriculture

His signs of civilization?

Air-conditioning and Novocain

Grew a rib, grew a woman

between these banks grown into hills

the sun's chaotic diadem uncomprehending

Hudson's gunmetal rib put down

Did he know she was off him? Looks asleep

Did she know it was neither of these things?

Eve is dancing to Eddie Kirkland

floats as a proto-continent

How little the molecules move

* * *

Chopping, chopping
The race as a concise dictionary of the afterlife
Rough shodding, faint dream of reason

Counting, counting
Fetal sectional anatomy
Grammar and the pelvis hold firm
. . . how the world perpetually ends
in Icarus and paradox

In love with
pain not understood
(marine regions, almanac, veil
mixed sins, a secret weight)

* * *

She is warm in the grass and he smiles. She can't believe her own face
as unshattered. Falling out stories as indifferent from fucking. The
bare lightbulb falls from the cord. Eve as apple. Knowledge as broken
information. Newton taps a force in disguise. Flee the charred bird. Fill
the pockets with fruit for the ride. Turn on the radio. Make wings from
two fields. Simple knowledge: how to breathe when ground flew into
the hands.

* * *

Horse-gallows, wind-tree
and the Prince of Air
Inch the limb
Tight umbilical twisting
Hung from a nine-night

Jump from a tree
Jumped off a hill first
Jumping from his cross and still tied to it
Keep the legs up
More than a messiah could bear
man with a rope swinging his shame upside down

Moved further out and balance
Oak bark until
rope caught cord, quiver
Can you pick up the feet, St. Peter?
Swing in the drunken darkness

Paralysis in a winter constellation
Tethered to taught and leap
The tree was absolutely willing
We've seen this before
What you didn't know is
Jumping with just a rope between his legs

* * *

Angels and oaks appear in May and June
as slender dropping clusters of catkins
Are often inconspicuous
Broken, brown shells
Yellow, bitter, usually inedible
Look for the old ones on the ground
Otherwise treated as uncuplike
slow-growing, long-lived

Boil out the tannins
Forests valued most for fattening pigs
Extensive browsing by cattle invites poisoning
Snowshoe, ruffed and sharptail, bobwhite
mourning, buckblack and browse twigs
Indians were acorns
acids removed by grinding and washing with hot water

The Anglo-Saxon rule in England:
anyone wantonly injuring or destroying an oak
should be fined accordingly

* * *

Mock crucifix or
the palace of suffering
(the room swims)
where plantain is ribgrass
When poetry is the carnival on the lawn
and the poem the carnage
"Pray for protection"
and prediction, simple algebra

It's a question of joy
of rib as river
Riverboat pilots
tell their stories
try to patent the solar system

Speedtrap:
house full of furniture
the optical quality of venetian blinds
Waking up from memory
the world as oracle
where dragonflies are "diamond needles"
where lacquer is red cabbage

* * *

A bare lightbulb hanging on its cord
       and pulls him close and
       then it went numb
       Assemble the vast abstractions above and below:
       bottles sewn beneath leaves in spring
       Collapse and inflate

Countried dump needled with unseamed
       bottles escape from the hands
       Eve crossed a biblical terrain
       Eve in the body of Dorcas
       Eve has crossed a starless sky

Eve has Orion by the belt buckle
       Gather the ancient unnecessary wheat above and below
       He found a cocaine heart
       He hangs from his feet by a nail
       mouth rusted shut by the sea
       Imperfection as death's bald invitation
       It's beautiful there

Kiss around the numb to discover
       Leave blood on the hands
       left for 300 years
       Medicine in a stone wall
       "Now no one can make you afraid
       of a minor world"

* * *

Fell on themselves shot down a narrow barrel

Only running. It was not a race

Unseen against the sky

"If you traveled these roads, there was trouble"

Narrow red road cut as a ring into a finger

Refugeed in Brittany

owls as burnt patches on the trees overhead

Servitude giving rise to expectant

Absence of architecture when they left

They were only playing

Take a wedding ring, cut it once, lay it flat

This is a road. This is a war

The ruin and run of things down a dirt road

"The roads were terrible, there was trouble"

A woman meeting hooves with the eye

Carts everywhere and no animals to pull them

The rifle pours a smothering grain

What did she carry toward her temporary house?

Whole life turned into a secret word

                              * * *

"Experience and speed have a
direct correlation to the risk
a driver faces at Daytona."
Stripped over time of its white
thoughtless cage, the body sleeps as speed

Stories recounted with rubbed hands
are things preferred as muted out

Beautiful under Plexiglas and unused
velocity as a recent type of snow
Unattainable movement aspired to
he is the rope run out if hands
tied to something heavy and falling

What is not left must be made up
Someone's mouth shakes me
Hair gathers a dirty ice
Accident as sacrament
Head bathed in the technical basin
Rub an inversion onto the back
and tie him there

* * *

Eden was a Kelvin palace

Of snow form a rib

Pool stick run up a wall

Sign of civilization simultaneous:

the rib and the woman

snow and the consideration of snow

"Solamente una juega, solamente una juega"

Steam rises off the water in the form of Eve

Subsequent indifference sunk into the ground

Swim off the side into

chlorine the color of a pool table

* * *

Two oil tanks collapse in Baltimore:
    Orion and Simon, hunting, fishing
    Once grammar existed only in his face
    Reward for laying 10 yards of indigenous slate
    Sliver of a man as an arc of soap

Stand them in coltsfoot and salt
    Sun rusting the junk sky
    The track rejects imperfection
    There is a live bird hung at her throat

To be a sword on the bottom of the ocean
    Become perfect at 200 miles an hour
    Pencil him in at the belt
    Fuck him at his rock

Razed at zero chassis
    Strafe the cash crop
    You are the boat that sails the water above me
    Where you are when the oil tanks
    What we all want:
    where feeling begins
    What is complete can vanish or be replicated
    Two people died on the asphalt circle
    Two people raked the hillside for bottles

Night

Science of fluids in motion

Cut the heart from the barn owl

Place it to the left of the sternum

There. She will tell you everything

Sleep is the sense to be done under:

the chisel's nude grave

"Destruction of the matter" between us

Disintegration of the driver's senseless form

Night about to be revised

                           * * *

Sing in the recent and overnight
Winter as the salt
abstraction of the sea
Slaves pushed a ferry
off the seasonal flats

I place a car key under the tongue
for the new year's ride
Your only rule:
"can't get off"

Ground appears every 12 hours
Boots to the edge
December's flat breath forms

brittle things
tidal speech

Visibility as an interior language

* * *

+1 accidental
Race vary from very to almost
Sex similar shrill rasping hiss or snore
The awe at the close is characteristic
Tree limit to Tierra del Fuego
(3) See Gyrefalcon (white phase)
Underwing: a black carpal
Unusually silent, also a repeated "rick"
Wail: tremulous descent into the pitch
Wooded river bottoms, wooded swamps
Woodland, thicket, grove

* * *

"By pure motions of its own"

a deer hooked to an iron fence

a ribbon, an unlit shirt

the hard bearings in the spine

"But that which dwells in heaven"

is bound until late February

Cut me from ice: moon off an ingot

Cut for one hour the number "2" from

and two letters

Float as the sun floats, belly up

Sky going under, tapping across the sea's opaque eye

* * *

A dirty sheet to keep the ice in

Allow the skin to part
Art as autopsy
as a sea of rust

Blood jumps through boxes on the paper
and blood hindrance
Glassy host in each fist
Graph the mood of the stalagmite
Grow a mask and eat it
Here is the list
Hypothermia as taking it all in

* * *

Lie in the sand. The sand is dusk beneath us. Cold. Sky rusts on its
rim. Precarious. There is one large tree, a monopoly. Bark of heaven.
Spruce against a darkening. Look and look for stars and none and none
appear. Panic and search his body for coals implied. Fear them to be in
your mouth (But you have not the genius for them to be there). Not
swallowed, but somewhere

* * *

Hung miracles and unsought

Hung now with an abstract paw, a doll's arm

This is the shape I have bought

Local tarnishing plain, tiny asbestos forest

A board of aluminum covers the bed

He cut the moon off an ingot

Remember, when photographing the Lotus

it may bite at the hands

"Rough hammer to the stubborn"

Saw thin scales off pipe

attach to swim the thick water

Shape of a bird

beveled from a dangerous commerce

* * *

Facial disks dwarf the yellow eyes
Emphatic, a sneezy bark
Eurasia, North Africa
Farms, barns, towns, cliffs
Female low in the pitch
Flight noiseless, mothlike
Frozen close to the trunk of a dense tree
Knock-kneed, pale, lengthwise on your belly
Map 188
Marshes fresh and salt
Muskeg pale horn-colored
nearly cosmopolitan of the open country
Open country often seen by day standing

Pale cinnamon underparts ghostly by night
Our only with a white burnt heart, a shaped face

* * *

Senseless form cannot tell

out the neck's muscular wire

She lies flat against time

I stare at the abdominal miracle

muscle of constant flux removed

Body unaware of the mask:

the scaffold of life

Garment, skin and several losses

Night loves the rivergod senseless

* * *

Promethium flows through the veins
Ice poured out of a red pitcher upstream
Raze a tongue of stones
jutted into the Hudson's mouth

Men the shade of the river:
the partials of bottles
The season is over
crops ungathered

". . . O blood, O wood"
Water tongues toward land

Yelverton's Landing
Who owned other men?
Yelverton was a man with a boat

Rock, ocher, whitewash
Windows sealed in prior text
"Sawmill, brickyard, store
Slaves sculled his ferry across the Hudson"

Water's rough throat threaded
with lumber, oil, rail
Mouth studded with broken
china, salt, jars, trunks, tarps
"It's a baby's arm
A doll's. Porcelain"
What the river gave

* * *

The theatre of panic and panic itself. Leave things behind. Tree of
indifference, tree of hope. The needling green, the complicated arms. And
the sky, an exploited ruin, a paint can in the fire: char, rust, gas. Wax the
cerecloth. Wrap the dead and place them up there to burn

* * *

"Since I was born, and such my father was"

Skate over and over this pond

"Stone gives human shape, now this"

circle-faced spreads cracks across

There is a certain illness to the sun

God at once origin and atheist

You made tools to cut the ice from the abdomen

There is a certain water against day's underbelly

"Thou alone are good, etc. "

Tucked in, navigation winters in a cradleboard

until nothing is left

What kind of a maker are you?

Hudson drowns under itself

Without handles, note how it bites the hand

Simply made tools from air

                              * * *

Ignore all warnings
in one suck breath

The origin of pulse
it interests them, the key under the tongue
90 minutes of mechanical absence
of occasion to fool yourself for

Plant the usual crop: report and sorrow
Rust breaks the harvest
Scalpel touched here

Singe a warning

Sewn as cure into the root
Surgery for pure mystery and crowd-control
Corn stalks bulging at the knuckle:
secrets taken back

The flying heart proves the cut
Either the winter of thought
or a cottoned halo

Off at 82 degrees
On the body out of interest

                                       * * *

Crow-sized adjacent meadows
also a catlike whine
also a harsh scream around Hudson Bay
Arctic, circumpolar
Belly obscurely
Birch scrub, tamarack bog
Bobs and bows when agitated
Canada to Honduras:
a conspicuous white-throated ground
Cyclic winter irruptions southward
Day-flying: posts, dunes, haystacks, etc.
Night distinguished in flight as dusk

Anne Gorrick lives in West Park, New York, and is a visual artist as well as a poet. Her poems have appeared in the journals *American Letters and Commentary, Fence, Gutcult, Shearsman,* and *Sulfur* among others. Collaborating with artist Cynthia Winika, she produced a limited edition artists' book, *"Swans, the ice," she said,* through the Women's Studio Workshop in Rosendale, New York. She curates the reading series, *Cadmium Text,* devoted to innovative writing in and around the Hudson Valley. She also co-curates the electronic journal *Peep/Show.*

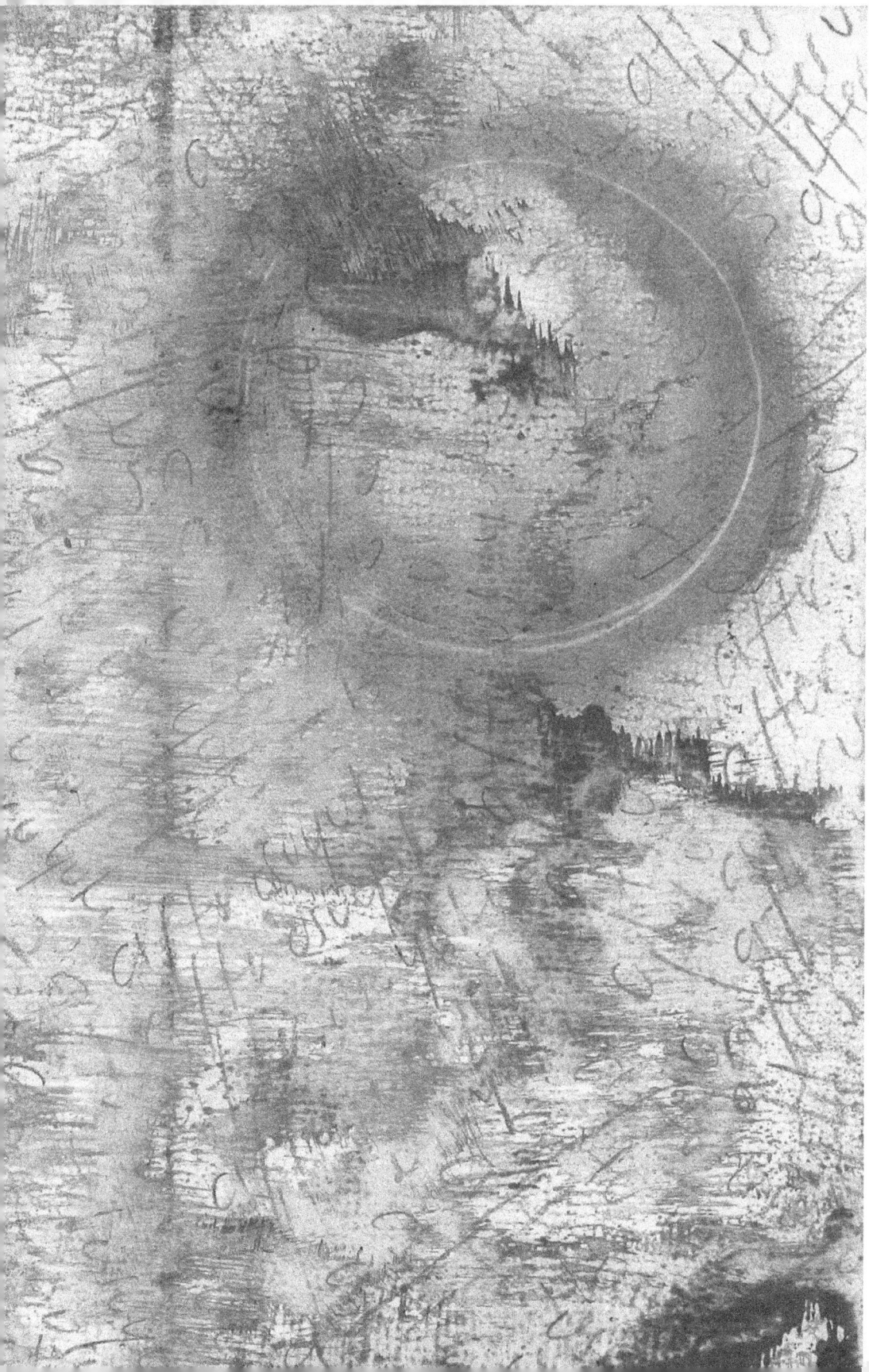

www.ingramcontent.com/pod-product-compliance
Lightning Source LLC
Chambersburg PA
CBHW022206080426
42734CB00006B/566